ANGKOR

ANGKOR

DAVID STANFORD

F

FRANCES LINCOLN LIMITED

PUBLISHERS

To my wife and family who, in everything I do, always encourage me with their love and understanding.

Frances Lincoln Ltd
4 Torriano Mews
Torriano Avenue
London NW5 2RZ
www.franceslincoln.com

Angkor
Copyright © Frances Lincoln Ltd 2009
Text and photographs © David Stanford 2009

First Frances Lincoln edition 2009

A catalogue record for this book is available from
the British Library

ISBN 978-0-7112-3044-6

Printed in Singapore

9 8 7 6 5 4 3 2 1

CONTENTS

———

Preface   6

Introduction   8

REDISCOVERY   10

PLAN OF ANGKOR   14

ANGKOR WAT   16

AYUTTHAYA   44

ANGKOR THOM   48

BANTEAY KDEI   56

THE BAYON   58

TERRACE OF THE ELEPHANTS   64

PRASAT SUOR PRAT   72

TERRACE OF THE LEPER KING   74

PREAH KHAN   78

TA PHROM   88

BANTEAY SREI   94

BANTEAY SAMRE   100

THE KLEANGS   100

PRASAT KRAVAN   101

KOBAL SPEIN   102

SCULPTURE   104

A note on religion   108

Glossary   110

Index   112

PREFACE

———◆———

Although it covers a vastly different subject from my three previous books on Suffolk, Essex and Norfolk churches, this book still falls very much in line with my long-standing interest in recording historical subject matter in photographs. All the photographs in this book were taken digitally and they were deliberately taken on lower-end digital cameras rather than on expensive high-end professional cameras. To those not interested in photography this will be of no consequence, but it was a singular condition of my agreeing to undertake my first project, *Suffolk Churches*, for Frances Lincoln, and I must commend their decision to give me free rein in my conviction that this was a realistic and professional way to proceed in the tough, competitive and expensive world of publishing, at a time when digital photography was far from where it is now. Since then, with the explosion in digital photography, their initial decision to take the risk has proved a wise one and my conventional film cameras now lie unused. During the last few years I have completed professional assignments in places as diverse as Ethiopia, Peru, Australia, France and Cambodia, using a variety of digital cameras, and, although I admit that in the early days

One of the staircases at Angkor Wat.

I cautiously covered everything on film as a kind of insurance policy, the digital results increasingly held up or surpassed that of film, and I have not used that medium for years now. None, save a few die-hard purists, will any longer identify digital photography as an inferior photographic process, and most people now view the digital world for what it is, simply another method of recording exciting images and ideas. No longer in its infancy, and evolving at an astonishing pace, the new techniques of working digitally can enhance what we see, placing at our disposal all manner of new experiences in the world of visual representation, but with one governing maxim, one that applies to all visual statements: nothing will make a bad picture good, no matter what the specifications of the equipment, methods or techniques used.

Many people will recognize Angkor from photographs; some may dream of visiting one day, and increasing numbers of people already have. But whether familiar or vaguely known, the massive scale and staggering history of the place cannot be viewed except with a sense of awe, so if this book goes any way towards conveying the scale, majesty and wonder of the place, it will have served its purpose and I will be content.

A monk strides away
from the Terrace of
the Elephants

INTRODUCTION

Full coverage of a site as large and complex as Angkor is well outside the scope of this book. That said, I can do no better, for those interested in a more detailed and learned analysis of the subject, than recommend a book which for my money is definitive. Maurice Glaize was curator of Angkor from 1937–46 and his *Les Monuments du groupe d'Angkor*, published in 1944, helps towards understanding the full significance and background of this incredible place. The fact that his book was written over sixty years ago takes nothing from it and anything that has been revealed by later research can easily be assembled and absorbed into the general description that Glaize painted all those years ago.

Les Monuments du groupe d'Angkor is a deeply researched and learned look at Angkor, illustrated with some excellent but necessarily limited black-and-white photographs. It is my hope to enhance the limitations of his images by the use of modern photographic technique. While his book was an in-depth work, mine is largely a visual tour in search of the ambiance of Angkor, and for this purpose I have concentrated not on the whole massive site but selected buildings within the complex: buildings, sculptures and other shots that I hope give convey a general feel of the whole.

The buildings I have chosen are possibly among the better known but not always the best understood, so with what text I feel absolutely necessary and leaving as much as possible to my pictures I have attempted not only to present this magical place in its full splendour but also, where I can, elucidate a little, while always continually fleeing back into the arms of Glaize for definitive backup.

An important note should be made here and that is that although Angkor ceased to be the capital of the Khmer civilisation in 1431, it was never deserted throughout the years that followed. It has always been a place of worship and remains so today. To many millions of Buddhists this is a holy shrine, but to many others it is simply a tourist attraction, something to be ticked off on a list of things to see. But this is a foolish and quite wrong notion for visiting it. The importance of this UNESCO World Heritage Site must be accepted not only for its historic, picturesque and curiosity value but also for the fact that it is a living place, a place that has survived the terrible tribulations of history, and yet a deeply spiritual place, which speaks of grandeur, yes, but also of faith and the devotion of countless millions for over well over a thousand years.

REDISCOVERY

The word 'rediscovery' is something of an exaggeration, for Angkor was never really lost. Since after its collapse and the end of the heady days of the mighty Khmer civilisation it ceased to play a part as a capital city, yet it continued as an important place of pilgrimage not just for Cambodians but for people from many far-flung places, including a few intrepid Europeans. To Western eyes, however, Angkor does owe its re-emergence from the past to the formidable efforts of a French adventurer-explorer named Henri Mouhot, who, while living in Jersey with his wife, a daughter of the famous explorer Mungo Park, stumbled across a book about Siam that fired him with an obsession to make an expedition there. Having obtained funds from, among others, the Geographical and Zoological Societies in London, he set out in 1858 on a botanical expedition of an area that was not only uncharted but largely unknown to the West. Over the next three years he conducted four extremely dangerous and daring journeys into the interiors of Siam, Cambodia and Laos. It was on the second of these expeditions in 1860 that he spent three weeks among the ruins at Angkor, studying them and piecing together their history with the wide-eyed enthusiasm characterised in his subsequent writings. As stated, he was by no means the first European to visit or write about this strange and magical place but he was by far the most enthusiastic, interesting and detailed commentator. Not always accurate in detail – for instance he was convinced that the ruins dated back several thousand years, although it was already known they were much later – he was nevertheless responsible for a huge upsurge in interest in the subject.

Sadly, by the time his book *Travels in Siam, Cambodia and Laos* was published in 1864, Mouhot was long dead of fever in the jungles of Laos. Even now extensive travel in the interior jungles of these countries is hard and not for the faint hearted, but at a time when practically nothing was known and certainly no reliable maps existed, Mouhot's adventures can only be viewed as either the ultimate in foolhardiness or sublime courage coupled with a perennial inquisitiveness. Mouhot might be seen as the perfect template for an adventurer-explorer on a mission, a template that would produce many other jungle wanderers, such as Colonel Fawcett, who in the next century disappeared into the matto grosso jungle of Brazil, searching for he knew not what, but searching just the same.

The tomb of Henri Mouhot on the banks of a tributary of the mighty Mekong River, near Luang Prabang, Laos

What Mouhot introduced to a wide-eyed Western world was a vast complex of temples spanning an area in excess of 70 square miles around the Cambodian town of Siem Reap, vast even by modern standards. Within that area there are over 100 temple sites, the remains of elaborate buildings built by successive Khmer kings spanning a period from the seventh to the fifteenth centuries AD. Nothing remains of the wood-built civic buildings and other habitations that constituted the city itself, and consequently our knowledge of the lives of the civilian population is scant. However, information gleaned from the many inscriptions found throughout the region, coupled with the obvious remains of a vast irrigation system indicate the sheer scale and complexity of the city. Dressed brick was mainly used for the early temples, then increasingly laterite, a rust-coloured mudstone, and finally sandstone, which was quarried mostly from the Kulen Hills, about 31 miles to the north-east of Siem Reap.

The religion of the Khmer people evolved from early animism through a form of Hinduism, eventually pivoting on a pragmatic co-existence between the varied tenets of Brahmanism and Buddhism. Two branches of the Buddhist faith, the Mahayana and the later Theravada schools, held sway but it is Mahayana, often referred to as the 'Greater Vehicle', that was at the centre of the concept of Angkor and the principles of this belief are expressed and celebrated in every aspect of the buildings, sculptures and decoration. Many of the buildings were built as 'temple mountains' or pyramids, symbolic of the cosmic Mount Meru of Hindu mythology. A five-tiered mountain at the centre of the universe, represented by the temple, was said to be encircled by seven chains of mountains, represented by the enclosure walls, which were surrounded in turn by the sea represented by the moat, and in general this pattern is echoed throughout the site with variations related to the actual period in which a particular building was erected.

Mahout himself spent only three, albeit intensively busy, weeks at Angkor and today if one wished to visit every single temple it would take at least that, if not longer.

Ruins within Ta Phrom

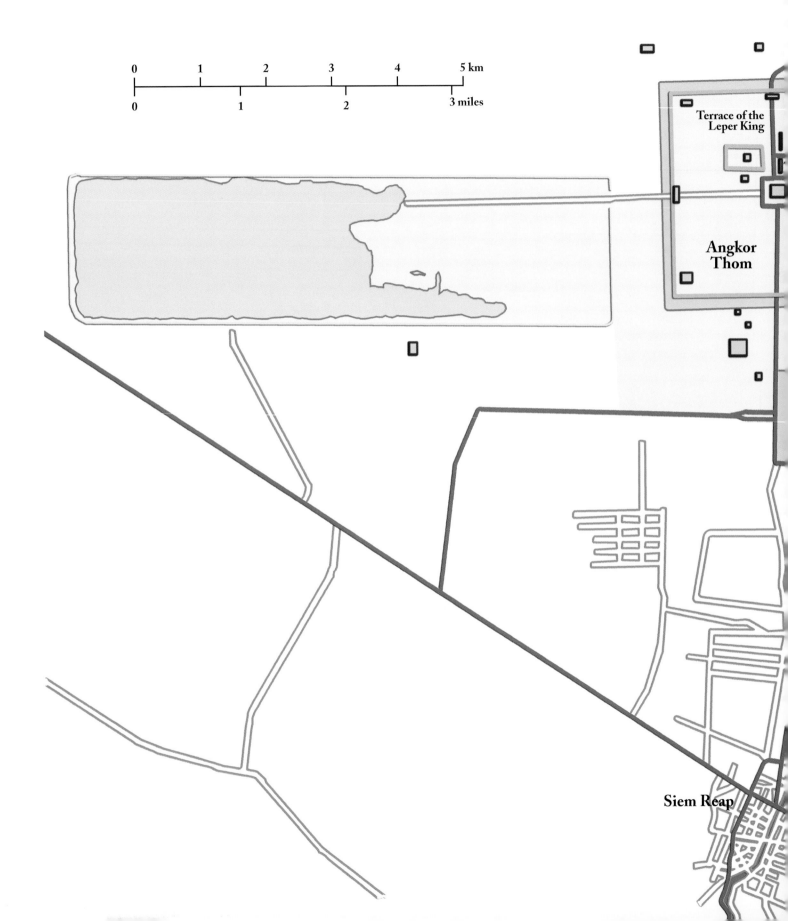

0   1   2   3   4   5 km

0   1   2   3 miles

**Terrace of the
Leper King**

**Angkor
Thom**

Siem Reap

Preah
Khan

Ta Phrom

Banteay
Kdei

Prasat
Kravan

Banteay
Samre

or Wat

PLAN OF ANGKOR

ANGKOR WAT

Angkor Wat, the best known and undisputed jewel in the crown of the entire Angkor site, is just one temple among the many spread over an area said to cover 250 square miles. The word wat, or sometimes, incorrectly, vat (which, in fact, can only be applied to temples in Laos), is nowadays often used as a generic term for any temple or temple ruins in Southeast Asia. However, in its strictest sense the word, which has its roots in Sanskrit, actually means a monastic school. In Cambodia, Thailand and Laos, wats were usually Buddhist devotional temples, with schools and resident monks operating not unlike medieval European monasteries and seminaries. Therefore, any such temple that does not house actively practising monks, their acolytes, students and novices should not correctly be referred to as a wat. However, in the language of modern Thailand, wat has come to mean any place of worship, except a mosque. For example, a 'wat krit' is a Christian church and a 'wat khaek' is a Hindu temple.

Angkor (derived from the Sanskrit word *nagara*, meaning 'city') was the ancient capital city of the Khmer empire situated just north of the Tonle Sap (great lake) near the town of Siem Reap. During the rainy season between May and October the Mekong River, unable to hold the extra water from melting snows and rain, spills over and more than doubles the size of Tonle Sap, forming a natural reservoir. Gradually the size and depth of the lake subsides until almost dry and then the cycle starts over again. With sluices, dams, reservoirs and canals, the Khmers used the natural feature of the Mekong's annual cycle in the remarkably sophisticated design of their city. This was a city built on water, designed to irrigate, feed and transport a population estimated at over a million, which is vast for that period in history. The magnificence and practicality of the city was described by a visiting Chinese envoy Zhou Daguan, who lived in the city for a year in the thirteenth century. Approached nowadays during the dry season, when most of the water has gone, it is hard to imagine a virtual Venice, but at the height of its glory that must have been what Angkor resembled.

Angkor Wat was built in the early twelfth century by the Cambodian King Suryavarman II as his state temple and quite possibly his mausoleum (although this

remains unproven). This is a relatively late date in the history of the Khmer empire, which flourished from the eighth century until the city's final demise in 1431. Many of the buildings within the site as a whole are much earlier than Angkor Wat, one of the earliest being Preah Ko, constructed in the ninth century.

With the construction of Angkor Wat, Suryavarman broke with the traditions and work of previous Khmer kings and, heavily influenced by the rise of Vaisnavism in India, dedicated this temple to Vishnu rather than to Shiva. The external plan of the building is an architectural representation of the basic tenets of Hindu cosmology, with the central towers representing Mount Meru, home of the gods, the outer walls representing the mountains enclosing the world, and the moat representing the oceans of the world. The geometry and measurements of this temple and its interrelated parts are all of great cosmological significance. This particular building is the largest and best-preserved temple within the Angkor complex, and the only one to have remained a significant religious centre and place of worship up to the present day, eventually evolving into a Buddhist temple. It is undoubtedly the best surviving example of the high classical style of Khmer architecture. Two extremely long causeways form the approach to the building, giving one ample time to absorb the sheer size of the construction the nearer one gets to its entrance, and any remaining water serves to remind you of its importance to the design of the city. Angkor Wat is surrounded on

The crowded causeway to Angkor Wat, 2007

each side by walls nearly half a mile long which enclose three rectangular galleries, each raised above the next and in the centre a rectangular arrangement of five towers, one at each corner and one rising above the others in the middle. Nothing is without deep religious meaning; as with medieval cathedrals, the story of the religion is told and celebrated within the very fabric of the building.

This temple is approached across a vast swathe of open ground, eventually leading on to a long causeway bridging a moat over 600 feet wide, making this one of the most spectacular approaches to any building in the world. The distant view of the temple across the causeway is simply stunning and as one gradually draws nearer the west entrance it forces a contemplative mood filled with anticipation of what wonders this temple will actually hold. There could be no better way to enter such an awesome place.

It is a matter of debate among scholars as to why, unlike any other Angkorian temple, Angkor Wat is approached from the west. It was obviously a matter of some symbolic significance, now long lost, but from a purely aesthetic point of view, it

Part of the inner
courtyard, Angkor
Wat

OPPOSITE
Decorative lions,
Angkor Wat

ABOVE AND LEFT
Details of naga
balustrades, Angkor
Wat

is hard to imagine a better positioning. In terms of an introduction to the site as a whole, it approaches the architectural sublime.

Khmer architecture emphasises the notion of axis and symmetry, using symbolism to convey deeply rooted religious beliefs, traditions and legends. Each temple was surrounded by a moat representing the world's oceans yet from a practical point of view this would also have provided an excellent means of defence. Across the moat extends a wide paved causeway, sometimes running for hundreds of metres, and bordered by balustrades set on stone blocks and at intervals 'dvarapalas' (lions armed with clubs) – another typically Khmer motif – stand as guardians.

As one walks across the causeways one almost feels watched by the nagas, cobra-like figures, sometimes with multiple heads, always in uneven numbers, from three to nine, arranged in a fan, that form the balustrade. These creatures play an important role in both Hindu and Buddhist mythology and seem to originate from pre-Aryan fertility cults in India. The nagas exist in an aquatic underworld and are thus a

personification of terrestrial waters as well
as serving as door and gate guardians. Due
to the great power they wield, they not only
protect the underworld but bestow fertility
and wealth on the specific area – such as
a field, a place of worship, or even a whole
country – with which they are associated.
If a naga is properly worshipped prosperity
will be the result. If ignored or slighted, they
will bring disaster. As the Buddha achieved
enlightenment he is said to have been
protected by the cobra hood of the nagaraja
Mucalinda, symbolizing the fact that the
nagas have placed their natural powers at the

service of the Buddha. All of this is plays a
large part in the legend of the Khmer people
and the entirely original motif of the naga
balustrade is of fundamental importance.

Like the Khmer priests, the architects
and sculptors were but servants of an all-
powerful religious and cultural tradition. Just
as countless nameless Christian craftsmen
had created cathedrals of extraordinary
beauty – Khmer craftsmen working within
strict boundaries of belief also carried out
their highly creative work with equal self
denial, their achievement also remaining
anonymous and impersonal. Working to an

Western façade of
Angkor Wat

abstract concept, they were subject to constant repetition – yet they achieved not monotony but rhythm.

As previously stated, the temple mountain is an important concept in the Hindu faith. The temples at Angkor were built as symbolic representations of Mount Meru. It is said that Mount Meru has its roots in hell and its summit in heaven. It is surrounded by seven rings of golden mountains, each separated from the other by one of seven circular oceans. The summit is crowned with a golden palace where Indra, king of the Hindu gods, resides. The whole of this superstructure rises from an even greater outer ocean, flanked by four main continents, each with two subcontinents. Water was seen not just as a life-sustaining element, but as a fundamental part of the religious

Eastern façade of
Angkor Wat

substance of all things, and so was an essential part of the floor plan used by the Khmer builders of Angkor Wat. For the Khmer people, the development of agricultural irrigation became inseparable from religious dogma, simply part of their wish to emulate that vision of heaven on earth.

The stepped terraces lining the causeways and main buildings carry religiously symbolic concepts into the human struggle for survival. During the dry season, when water quickly disappeared, cattle could (and still do) graze and fertilize these lush open-terraced spaces, and as soon as the rains came, those same spaces filled with water just as quickly. This in turn provided all-important waterways for transportation and the rapid rotation of rice crops and fish – a

perfect ecosystem. It is no mere coincidence nor simple artistic embellishment that everywhere there are steps down to summer lawns, whose usefulness became even more paramount when they became seasonal lakes.

As the Hindu religion found its way from India to Cambodia it is as though the traditional Indian ghats were transported with it and, as Hinduism mutated into Buddhism, the wisdom of these seasonal waterways continued as an integral part of the religion, which was really to become a way of life.

OPPOSITE
Corner detail of
exterior terrace,
Angkor Wat

ABOVE
Covered walkway,
Angkor Wat

Cloister, Angkor Wat

Having walked along the causeway and entered through the impressive porch that forms the main entrance to this mysteriously layered building, you find yourself in a completely enclosed internal quadrangle. Forming a new raised tier inside the external elevation of the building, this new area constitutes the second level of experience *en route* to the towers, the tops of which can occcasionally be seen lying much deper within the complex, towering high above everything else. Although the surrounding landscape can still be glimpsed through the open window slats of the quadrangle, this only serves to remind one that we are gradually leaving the physical world for the more transient world of the spirit.

Off to the right stretches the Gallery of a Thousand Buddhas and, to the left, the Hall of Echoes, both disappearing into the

An inner courtyard at
Angkor Wat

bowels of this inner construction. Throughout Angkor Wat flights of steps lead off in various directions. It has been suggested that these steps serve a greater purpose than that of a mere means of ascending to different levels, for often they seem unnecessary. But in mounting any one of these sets of stairs of ever-varying size and functionality one is forced to look upward. The eye is being continually guided upwards towards heaven.

Repetition is fundamental to the concept of everything you see at Angkor. It lies at the core of the design of each building, and can be seen clearly in the juxtaposition of each element. From the actual

ABOVE AND OPPOSITE
Apsaras decorating
the walls of the upper
floors, Angkor Wat

buildings themselves, through to the walls that are covered in low relief depictions of spiritual dogma set alongside key moments in Khmer history, all surrounded by myriads of dancing apsaras.

These, nymphs, usually carved in relief, are always portrayed bare-breasted and invariably in postures of classical Khmer dance. The apsara is not a goddess, yet neither is she a mere mortal. She is a celestial dancer who inhabits the kingdom of heaven that Angkor Wat mirrors on earth, and as such she represents Khmer maxims of ideal feminine beauty.

Confusion sometimes arises between the apsara and the deva

(or devetas). There are, in fact, no similarities, either in function or form. The traditional symbolism and appearance of the apsara is as outlined above. However, the cult of the devaraja permeates the whole site. Deva is a very ancient traditional Hindu term, albeit one that has mutated, by erroneous connection, into other languages. In English, a diva is female superstar with an outstanding vocal ability. To a Hindu worshipper, a deva is quite simply a deity, and a devetas a lesser deity, somewhat akin to a guardian angel.

Once inside the main body of the temple, you gain a true feel of the size, layout and orientation of the building, as well as of the relationship between the various projections and their surrounding

jungle. As an initial experience, before attempting to explore the labyrinthine lower levels, seek out one of the many higher vantage points. Using one of these commanding positions as a starting point gives an invaluable introduction to the structure as a whole and leads to a greater appreciation when one descends to explore the interiors at the lower levels.

Just as the long, deliberately languorous approach along that impressive causeway fills one with awe as the entrance gets closer, the sheer scale of the concept as a whole is accentuated when first

View from the upper level as seen from the position of the novice on the previous page

The windows at the upper levels look out across Angkor Wat to the four points of the compass

viewed from above. It is impresssive enough to a modern mind accusomed to the tools, equipment and building techniques of the modern world, but to the mind and senses of a twelfth-century Cambodian peasant it must have seemed that this truly was a reflection of the heaven their religion promised they were ultimately, after necessary purifying reincarnations, destined for. If Vishnu ever chose to reside on earth it would have to be here, for this was a true replica in miniature of the universe, a model of the cosmic world, an abode for the gods.

Towers surrounding
the central Mount
Meru tower with
ascending staircases,
interior of Angkor Wat
complex

Terrace featuring
bobbin windows,
Angkor Wat

BELOW
Apsaras on the lower
levels alongside
bobbin window struts,
Angkor Wat

Apsaras and window
details overlooking
a courtyard, Angkor
Wat

Bobbin windows and
walkway, Angkor Wat

Hall of Buddhas,
Angkor Wat

Active shrines deep
within the Angkor Wat
complex

Apsaras from various
points within and
around Angkor

AYUTTHAYA

THAI CAPITAL

Cambodia's relationship with its close neighbour Thailand has not always been friendly. Indeed, the final demise of Angkor was the direct result of a Thai invasion launched from the then Thai capital Ayutthaya.

The first Thai state is traditionally considered to have been the kingdom of Sukhothai, which was founded in 1238, and thrived for a relatively short period. In 1350, Sukhothai's power was overtaken by the much larger city state of Ayutthaya (named after the Indian city of Ayoda, the city of the hero Rama in the Hindu epic *Ramayana*), founded by King Ramathibodi. The Ayutthaya kings were not only Buddhist kings who ruled according to the dharma, but they were also devaraja, god-kings whose sacred power was associated with the Hindu gods Indra and Vishnu. To many Western observers, the kings of Ayutthaya were treated as if they were gods. The Frenchman Abbé de Choisy, who came to Ayutthaya in 1685, wrote that 'the king has absolute power, no one dares speak his name'. Bearing this in mind it must have been foremost in the minds of the Thai rulers to outdo the Angkorian achievement. To do this they were forced to copy certain aspects. The state religion changed to Theravada Buddhism, but the close proximity of the awesome city of Angkor proved an irritant to the Thais, since its grandeur continually undermined their own achievements.

The growth of Ayutthaya had coincided with the decline and eventual fall of the Khmer empire during the thirteenth to fifteenth centuries. The Thais had invaded Cambodia on numerous other occasions but never quite managed to hold on to what they conquered. In 1431, after a long siege, they sacked and looted Angkor, finally forcing the Cambodians to desert it and make Phnom Penh their capital. Sadly, after this invasion, Angkor never regained its status as the Khmer capital city and it was slowly consumed by the jungle. Yet it never ceased to exert its religious presence on those who actually saw it. Even this final fifteenth-century invasion failed to settle and colonize, and each time their invading armies returned back home, the Thais took with them much inspiration from Angkorian culture, especially in the field of architectural design.

Today a visit to Ayutthaya, some 50 miles north of modern Bangkok, reveals

The ancient Thai capital of Ayutthaya, north of modern Bangkok

many similarities with Angkor. For instance, the Thais chose to surround their city with water, eventually having three palaces and over 400 temples on the island city this formed. All this was threaded, as at Angkor, by a series of canals, but it never rivalled Angkor in scale. Another principal feature adapted from Angkor by the Thais is the frequent use of tall richly ornamented towers known as 'prangs'.

Eventually Ayutthaya suffered an even more vicious fate than Angkor. Over the years Thailand had been invaded no less than twenty-three times by the Burmese. In 1767, after a fifteen-month siege, the Thai capial fell and was sacked by a particularly vicious Burmese army out to destroy not adapt, learn or emulate anything Thai. The damage was on a far greater scale than the Thais had perpetrated on Angkor. From what was left one can now glean valuable insights not only about Ayutthaya but also about Angkor. For instance, the ruins at Ayutthaya have in many places lost their stone dressing, revealing a red-brick underbuilding that can be seen in some of the more dilapidated buildings at Angkor. Was this a technique exported to Ayutthaya by the retreating Thais?

LEFT
Terraces and
carvings destroyed
by the Burmese.
Note the undressed
brickwork structure

ANGKOR THOM

—◦◦∞◦◦—

THE GREAT CITY

Angkor Thom lies about a mile north of the entrance to Angkor Wat, its walls forming a square of 3½ square miles, by any standard a vast metropolis.

Whereas Angkor Wat is purely a religious complex, Angkor Thom, although also housing religious buildings, was a royal and secular city, the name deriving from the Sanskrit meaning 'great city'. What we see today was not the first city founded on this site. The earliest dated from the early tenth century but was completely remodelled and rebuilt by Jayavarman VII in the early thirteenth century. Jayavarman's new city was set at a slightly different orientation from the previous design and on a deliberately smaller, more self-contained scale. Building was undertaken with a close eye on defence since the warlike Chams had attacked and invaded the previous cities frequently. Jayavarman had only just ousted them and brought the area back under complete Cambodian control.

Angkor Thom was certainly grander than any European city of the period and with a population thought to number more than a million, at that time by far the most populous in the world. The only other comparable civic complex on earth was the Mayan city of Tikal in present-day Guatemala. Like Angkor Wat, the general layout and design of Angkor Thom adhered to the traditional concept of the 'Celestial City', a theme that predominated Khmer construction and the now-famous Bayon temple, representing the mythical Mount Meru, was placed at the epicentre of the new city. It was surrounded by 25-foot-high laterite walls and was entered through highly idiosyncratic gates known as gopuras, which would once have had massive wooden doors, each approached by a huge causeway spanning a navagable moat over 300 feet wide. The construction and design of these gopuras, dominated as they are on every projection by huge majestic stone faces, has become one of the most instantly recognizable pieces of Angkorian iconography.

The walls of the city are divided by two axes running north–south and east–west, and each wall is pierced by a gopura. An additional gopura, known as the 'Gate of Victory', pierces the east wall, north of the gopura known as the 'Gate of the Dead'. This fifth gateway led directly to the terraces of the royal palace and was probably used for ceremonial royal processions. It is worth noting that since the palace was constructed

Details from the gopuras and causeways, Angkor Thom

of wood only the stone foundations remain to be seen today. The
best-preserved gopura – thanks to the restoration work carried out
by Maurice Glaize, and undoubtedly now the most fascinating way
to enter this complex – is the southern one. Like the others it is
approached across a causeway on each side of which are large stone

Southern causeway
approach to Angkor
Thom

Southern causeway approach to Angkor Thom

figures engaged in the famous Hindu legend 'The Churning of the Ocean of Milk'. On the left side as you approach, fifty-four devas (guardian gods) tug at the head of the snake Shesha, while opposite on the right hand side fifty-four asuras (demon gods) tug at the snake's tail.

ABOVE
One of the four
cardinal point
gopuras leading to
Angkor Thom

RIGHT
The main gopura
leading to Angkor
Thom

Partially
reconstructed figures
on an Angkor Thom
causeway

Enigmatic faces
from one of the
causeways leading to
Angkor Thom

BANTEAY KDEI

THE CITADEL OF MONKS' CELLS

Little is known about this mysterious temple. There are absolutely no records of why, when or by whom it was built, and no inscriptions explaining anything about its history have yet been found. The designation as a 'citadel of monks' cells' carries little weight and does not necessarily prove that this was its function. What seems certain is that Banteay Kdei evolved around the same time as Angkor Wat from a small relatively unimportant site into a large central temple with sprawling clusters of buildings surrounded by a wall and decorative gopuras. There are striking similarities between this temple and Angkor Wat but a comparison can also be made with temples in Thailand, such as Phimai. The tragedy of Banteay Kdei is that for some inexplicable reason it was built using a very inferior grade of sandstone and this, coupled with illogical design changes during construction and uncharacteristically shoddy building techniques, has led to time taking a heavy toll.

The gate is in better condition than a lot of the complex and has some fine carving as do a number of the interior buildings so the site is well worth a visit.

BELOW
Detail of carvings
on the gopura and
surrounding wall,
Banteay Kdei

THE BAYON

ENIGMATIC FACES

Built on the traditional principle of temple-mountain, the Bayon, with its sea of over 200 gigantic faces looking in all directions, each with an enigmatic smile, is an instantly recognizable image of Angkor, as familiar as Angkor Wat itself. In fact, many people probably assume that the faces are an integral part of Angkor Wat rather than a feature of an entirely separate temple.

Built in the twelfth century by Jayavarman VII as part of his massive expansion of Angkor Thom, the Bayon is deliberately placed at the exact centre of the royal city and rises through three storeys to a height of around 140 feet. The lower floors are a pantheon of Khmer gods, but in reality this is a Buddhist temple that, during a period of transition from Hinduism to Buddhism as the state religion, retained large elements of Hindu imagery and cosmology. The upper terrace represents the completion of the of the religious transition for here there is no longer a vestige of Hindu belief. Here are the famous 'face towers', each of which supports two, three or four gigantic smiling faces. In addition to the mass of the central tower, smaller towers are located along the inner gallery, at the corners, entrances and

chapels on the upper terrace. 'Wherever one wanders,' wrote Maurice Glaize, 'the faces of Lokesvara follow and dominate with their multiple presence.' (Avalokitesvara, in Sanskrit, literally 'Lord who Looks Down', the bodhisattva who embodies the compassion of all Buddhas, also known as Lokesvara, 'Lord of the World', is the most widely revered bodhisattva in Buddhism and in Tibet is said to be incarnated in the Dalai Lama.) With religious transition accomplished, the

Monumental structures of the interior temple of the Bayon

principal religious image became a statue of the Buddha, 12 feet tall,
located in the santuary at the heart of the massive central tower. The
Buddha was portrayed seated in meditation, shielded from the elements
by the flared hood the serpent king Mucalinda. However, during the
reign of the Hindu restorationist monarch Jayavarman VIII (1243–95)
the figure was removed from the sanctuary and smashed to pieces. After
being recovered in 1933 from the bottom of a well, it was pieced back
together and is now on display in a small pavilion at Angkor.

Attempts to read some significance into the numbers of towers
and faces have met with the obstacle that these numbers have not
remained constant over the years. More towers have been added through
construction and others lost in decay. At one point there were thought
to have been forty-nine such towers of which only thirty-seven now

A glimpse through a
doorway at one of the
myriad faces of the
Bayon

remain. Today we see around 200 faces, but since some of these are only partially preserved there can be no definitive count. Opinions vary as to who the faces actually represent. One school of thought says they represent the god Avalokitesvara. Others posit that, since it is known he thought he was a bodhisattva, they are likenesses of Jayavarman VII himself. Whatever the facts, this is a unique and impressive place not just now, as an important and fascinating historical ruin but also in its heyday.

Zhou Daguan, the Chinese emissary to Cambodia in 1296–7, provides the only first-hand account of the splendour of Angkor Thom.

Remains of the external terrace surrounding the Bayon complex

Details of towers
constructed with
faces, the Bayon

OVERLEAF
Just a few of the
myriad faces that
comprise the Bayon

He wrote: 'At the centre of the Khmer kingdom rises a golden tower, the Bayon, flanked by more than twenty lesser towers and several hundred stone chambers. On the eastern side is a golden bridge guarded by two lions of gold, one on each side, with eight golden Buddhas spaced along the stone chambers.' In another passage, he describes a royal procession consisting of soldiers, numerous servant women and concubines, ministers and princes, and finally, 'the sovereign, standing on an elephant, holding his sacred sword in his hand'. As an official of the Chinese court he would have been used to grandeur, but his writing on Angkor makes no attempt to conceal the sense of awe that he felt.

TERRACE OF
THE ELEPHANTS

With a dedicated road running from the Gate of Victory to the central point of the terrace, the Terrace of the Elephants (as it it now known) extends from the temple known as the Baphuon to the Terrace of the Leper King. It is unclear today whether there was always a space between them. Alterations were evidently made to these structures over the centuries. Jayavarman VII had this huge platform attached the royal palace Phimeanakas (of which only a few ruins remain) for use in public religious ceremonies, grand audiences and for reviewing parades of his triumphant Khmer troops when they returned from their various campaigns. Stretching for about 400 yards the terrace was therefore an extremely important feature of the walled city of Angkor Thom.

Five staircases, three in the centre and one at each end, lead up to stepped platforms the lower enclosed by naga balustrades. At the centre of the highest terrace is a rostrum with more elephants and a lotus seats. The stairways are decorated with three-headed elephants carved in sandstone. Still more elephants along with thier mahouts cover most of the eastern face of the containing wall in the centre of which is a large Garuda accompanied by lions. The whole structure is a mass of carvings portraying hunting scenes with lions and tigers and further bas-reliefs depcting images of sporting events, such as wrestling, chariot racing and, interestingly, polo, a game now played all over the world but first played in Persia as a training game for cavalry units (sometimes with as many as a hundred players a side), usually the king's bodyguard or other elite troops. Could it be that this was the main purpose of the game among the Khmer people?

Detail of the Terrace of the Elephants

Steps to the royal platform, Terrace of the Elephants

Detail showing carving and construction of the Terrace of the Elephants

ABOVE
Wall frieze, Terrace of the Elephants

LEFT
Garudas incorporated into the walls of the terraces

Details of the
exquisite carvings to
be see in the Terrace
of the Elephants

Steps to the royal
platform, Terrace of
the Elephants

Wall of Garudas,
Terrace of the
Elephants

PRASAT SUOR PRAT

TEMPLE OF THE TIGHTROPE WALKER

Twelve red-brick towers stand facing the Terrace of the Elephants a short distance across open grass. There is little agreement as to the function of these buildings. They are generally thought to have been constructed by King Indravarman VII in the early thirteenth century but the fact that they are in a totally different style from anything else in the surrounding area has led some to suggest they were constructed pre-Bayon, possibly as early as the eleventh century. What is unanimously agreed is that they are Buddhist in origin. But where they fit into the scheme of things Angkorian is a matter of conjecture.

Lying to the east of the royal plain and built either side of a path leading to the Gate of Victory could equally suggest a ceremonial or a purely decorative purpose. There isn't even any real information as to the name. But there is an interesting story, dubious certainly, from Zhou Daguan. He writes in his classic *Customs of Cambodia* that these towers were used to settle legal disputes or matters of criminal justice. The accused or opposing parties were locked inside one of the towers. If they emereged in ill health, they were declared to have lost or found guilty, as decided by deivine decree. He does not mention how long they stayed locked up before eventually succumbing to illness.

Prasat Suor Prat, opposite the Terrace of the Elephants

TERRACE OF
THE LEPER KING

At the end of the Terrace of Elephants in the north-west corner of the royal square lies the famous Terrace of the Leper King. Built in the late twelfth century by Jayavarman VII in the Bayon style, its modern name is due to a fifteenth century sculpture discovered on the site. Some think the statue actually depicts the Hindu god Yama, god of death, and there is even some speculation that this spot was used as a royal cremation site. Discolouration due to moss and michen growing on the original statue has made it resemble a person with leprosy, hence its present name 'the Leper King'. This name becomes even more apt when the statue is associated with the Cambodian legends of at least two Angkorian kings having had leposy. We do know, however, the name by which the Cambodians knew the statue, as it was etched at the bottom of the original statue. They knew him as Dharmaraja.

Some 23 feet high, the structure forms a terrace above walls covered with carved nagas, demons and hosts of mythological creatures. There is also a long low trench or corridor, the inner wall of which, also covered in carvings, is earlier than the outer wall, only having been excavated in the 1990s by French archaeologists. Debate continues regarding who the statue on the upper terrace actually represents, but most modern scholarship suggests it is a combination of Jayavarman VII and Buddha, and that this was probably the site of the royal crematorium.

Whoever he is, he now sits upon a platform at the top of the structure gazing enigmatically ahead, huge yet sexless, hauntingly regal, when draped in saffron cloth by the adoring locals.

LEFT BELOW
The Leper King, an
unlikely but still active
shrine

Carvings on the wall
of the Terrace of the
Leper King

Detail of wall surrounding the Terrace of the Leper King

PREAH KHAN

THE SACRED SWORD

It was as recently as 1989 that the Cambodian government, in conjunction with the World Monuments Fund, started work on reconstructing and making sense of what was, at that time, mainly a rubble-strewn group of buildings constituting Preah Khan. Even now it remains devoured by the surrounding jungle in places, though not to the same extent as Ta Phrom, the Angkorian complex with which Preah Khan has the most similarities in style. Over the years, the work of clearing and restoring has revealed the real importance and signficance of this site.

Built by Jayavarman VII in 1191 as a monastery and centre of Buddhist learning, Preah Khan forms a rectangle 750 × 875 yards, covering an area of 138 acres surrounded by moats. In accordance with the formula adopted in Jayavarman VII's time, all the most important elements of the site are compressed into a relatively small space. In fact, most of its buildings of major significance are situated within the central enclosure which measures only 200 × 220 yards.Outside this very compact area lie further randomly placed buildings, such as the Pavilion and the Dharmasala, and these in turn would probably have been surrounded by a vast area of habitation covered with huts and timber houses, long since disappeared. Interestingly, Maurice Glaize felt that the many short inscriptions extolling pious foundations, and naming equally numerous idols representing deified dignitaries, gave the whole complex the character of a temple of remembrance. In 1939 a 7-foot stone stele was discovered. Richly inscribed on all four sides it revealed much of the day-to-day life of the temple and, incidentally, pointed out that the whole area on which Preah Khan stands was the site of a battle in which Jayavarman VII finally and comprehensively defeated the Chams. The inscriptions also throw a clear light on the

Causeway leading to
Preah Khan

name of the monastery, since they refer to Preah Khan as Nagara Jayasri, or 'The City of the Sacred Sword'. Also among the inscriptions is a list of the monastery's 139 annual feast days and a sort of 'mission statement', regarding the purpose and function of the monastery.

The site is best approached from the east along the imposing processional way, which leads over the original moat. This causeway, like others at Angkor, is lined with gods and demons and leads to the outer gopura. Through this gate lies a long avenue bathed in sparkling sunlight bursting through the foliage. If it were not for the tropical weather this could almost be a Parisian park setting. The avenue is lined with carved stone lanterns, sadly defaced, missing their

Details from the interior of the Preah Khan complex

representations of the Buddha, which were removed by zealots in their attempt to transform this confirmedly Buddhist complex into a Hindu temple. There are similar entrances to the north and south but these lack the grandeur of an avenued approach and are simply gopura gates. Approaching the central temple areas you pass walls bearing huge sandstone carvings of Garuda, the mythical Hindu bird. Sixty-eight of these carving spand the surrounding walls at 115-foot intervals. These are the guardians of Preah Khan.

To the east stands the Dharmasala, a beautiful structure looking like nothing so much as a piece of delicious confectionary. It was once thought to be a pilgrims' rest house, but modern scholarship has now identified it as more probably a small temple housing the sacred flame. The path eventually leads to a platform from which you can view the spectacular third gopura to the east, which comprises five entrances leading into the heart of the temple precinct. The large central tower was the royal entrance. All of the external walls of this group of buildings are covered with a huge variety of bas relief carvings and other decorative features. Once through the arch one enters the Hall of Dancers, so named for the fabulous carved lintels depticting groups of celestial dancers.

To the north of the Hall of Dancers there lies a very strange structure: the Pavilion. This is a two-storey building, of classical European proportions, with tiers of round columns unlike any others at Angkor. According to legend it once housed the Preah Khan, or sacred sword. Shrine follows shrine as you work your way through this holy of holies to the western portico, where once the stone stele stood. Exiting to the north you are led through temples dedicated to Shiva, while exiting the site to the west takes you through the world of Vishnu, with various shrines dedicated to that god's many incarnations, including the ninth as Buddha. Interestingly, it is within this part of the complex that the only examples of painted stucco in the whole of the Angkor region are to be found. There is also evidence that after royal patronage left Angkor for good in the fifteenth century, this Vishnu temple continued to be used.

Details from
the Preah Khan
causeways

Dharmasala, Preah
Khan

Details from interior
of Preah Khan

Reconstructed naga
balustrade

One of the seventy-two Garudas on the walls of Preah Khan

TA PHROM

THE ANCESTOR BRAHMA

Once called Rajavihara Ta Phrom, which translates as 'The Ancestor Brahma', is for many the archetypical lost jungle temple, and was used as a setting in the 2001 film *Tomb Raider*. Yet in its heyday, Ta Phrom was a very important part of Angkor, the royal monastery. It was built by Jayavarman VII in honour of his mother in 1186, several years prior to the construction of the other monastery, dedicated to his father, at Preah Khan.

Ta Phrom has, except for path clearing and essential structural securing, been left in the same state for centuries. It is a total ruin, yet a place of great beauty, as if the contradictory nature of Shiva the destroyer and restorer, now rules here. The beauty and symbolism that was once created by man has through a virtual osmosis been transformed by nature into something altogether different.

Standing to the east of Angkor Thom, Ta Phrom is in fact one of the largest mountains in the Angkor region. Silent, serene and beautiful in the early morning, set deep inside its precincts, gigantic roots of banyan and kapok trees probe walls and terraces, forcing their way into crevices and under stones, turning everything in fantasy. Stone pillars are strangled by the weaving trunks and vegetation, which in turn have become supports for the crumbling architecture.

Much of the information we have regarding Ta Phrom comes from a Sanskrit inscription found carved inside the complex. Probably exaggerated for sycophantic reasons, it records some 3,140 incorporated villages and states that it took 79,365 people to maintain the temple, including 18 great priests, 2,740 officials, 2,202 assistants and 615 dancers. It also gives an inventory of property belonging to the temple, consisting of a set of golden dishes weighing more than half a tonne, 35 diamonds, 40,620 pearls, 4,540 precious stones, 876 veils from China, 512 silk beds and 523 parasols. Further details state that there were 39 towers with pinnacles and 566 groups of residences, as well as 260 statues of gods.

Entering through the eastern gopura, one can see the remains of a small part of the orginal laterite wall which once ran 650 × 1,100 yards around the complex. On the other side of this gate, after a short walk, is an elevated terrace, beyond which lies the next gopura – the inner eastern gopura. It has a cruciform tower with a pillared interior, four wings and two passages to the sides. The walls

Ta Phrom is a
complex devoured by
vegetation

of these passages are decorated with relief carvings. In general, Ta Phrom comprises a series of long low buildings standing on on level, with the centre of the monument reached by a series of towers connected by a series of galleries and passages. There is also a Hall of Dancers, which was probably used for ritual performances. Although it is now too unsafe to enter, its decoration can be glimpsed. Further west in the central area, another series of galleries and shrines present themselves. One gallery has some remains of Buddhist imagery in shallow niches, but most were destroyed during the religious reaction of the thirteenth century. Across a large surrounding courtyard with vegetation-capped towers, lies another sanctuary with a reclining Buddha.

Vegetation becomes part of the structure of Ta Phrom

The galleries of the southern tower also contain important carvings, including a group of divinities holding the hooves of Prince Siddartha's horse in order to muffle their sound during the grand departure of the future Buddha. Another gopura, with three towered passageways, has extensive sculpted devetas, while a lone dvarapala, armed with a huge club, guards yet another entrance. Excavation revealed a 4-foot-high sculpted plinth, completely buried. This square pillar was possibly the support for a small lightweight altar. The walls of the galleries are covered in sculpture, like a continuous embroidery. By contrast, the central sanctuary is remarkably plain, although the masonry is hammered, which may mean it was once painted and gilded. On leaving the northern part of this courtyard by its eastern gallery – after having first stopped to admire the finesse of the devetas

Massive trees thrive throughout Ta Phrom

Ruins of a temple
cloister, Ta Phrom

on its wall – you pass through a door that is eerily framed by the roots of a gigantic tree. Through another small door in one courtyard lies a gallery with a double row of pillars. Here we find one of the best known images of Ta Phrom: a whole architectural structure held in the grasp of tree roots, which grow up and through the vaulting, making it appear suspended from the limbs of a massive sleeping monster, whose tentacles encircle it and hang to the ground. Leaving this compound across the moat via another cruciform causeway, on which there are the reamins of some naga balustrades, a more visible sky provides a contrast to that slight claustrophobia of the extraordinary vegetable kingdom behind. From there, a 380-yard jungle track leads to the final western, and best-preserved, gopura, its top formed by the four faces of Lokesvara, where one exits into the real world.

BANTEAY SREI

THE CITADEL OF WOMEN

This astonishing pink temple complex dedicated to the Hindu god Shiva was only rediscovered in 1914. In 1923 it was the scene of the infamous Angkor art theft, when the French art historian and culturist André Malraux stole four devatas from it. He was eventually arrested and more than lucky to be released with a simple telling-off and their return. The irony was that the incident fired international interest in Angkor as a whole and stimulated restoration.

Significantly, this is the only major temple at Angkor not built by or for a king. Completed in AD 967 it was originally constructed by Yajnyavahara, a Brahmin counsellor of King Rajendravarman. The temple was named Tribhuvana Mahesvara ('Great Lord of the Threefold World') after the central shrine image, a Shaivite linga, and the town of Isvarapura grew up centred around the holy buildings. Expanded in the eleventh century, it finally came under the control of the king, who promptly changed the dedication, but an early twelfth-century inscription states that the temple was eventually given to the priest Divarakapandita, who rededicated it to Shiva. Generally thought to refer to the exquisitely delicate carving and decoration throughout, the modern name Banteay Srei translates as 'Citadel of the Women' or 'Citadel of Beauty'. This delicate intricacy of decoration was made possible by the use of soft pink sandstone. The wealth of decoration juxtaposed with the scale of the buildings and the wonderful pink coloured glow throughout puts one in mind of some ancient Indian cities. Indeed, the strong link between early Indian art and that of the Khmer people of this people is nowhere more apparent in Angkor than at this temple. The similarities between Banteay Srei and the much later Thai city of Ayutthaya might also be noted as a further example of the constant transmigration of religious styles.

BELOW
Details of pink sandstone carvings at Bateay Srei

RIGHT
Carved temple, Banteay Srei complex

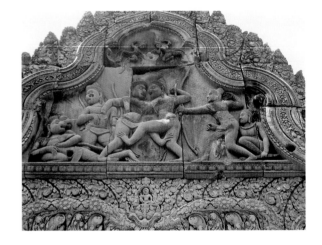

As with most Khmer temples, Banteay Srei is oriented to the east, but its fourth eastern gopura is all that remains of the walls of the original citadel and through the arch of this lies the processional way, lined with decorative markers and flanked by buildings. After the scale of the other sites in Angkor, this complex seems small and compact. Glaize's description of it as a 'caprice' is not inapt: the tightness of its construction, the deliberately narrow alleys and the openness of the sky make one feel as if right inside a delicious confectionary treat.

As a comparison in scale, Banteay Srei's outer wall covered an area totalling only 600 square yards, the causeway is a mere 220 feet long

Complete temple within Banteay Srei complex

Courtyard of library
buildings, Banteay
Srei

and the inner enclosure a mere 30 square yards – tiny in comparison
to the other sites. Yet everything contained in the larger sites is
represented within the enclosure, including two libraries, one in the
south-eastern corner and another in the north. The pediments of both
libraries are exquisitely carved. Those of the south library both feature
Shiva – the eastern pediment showing Ravana shaking Mount Kailish,
with Shiva at the summit, and the pediment to the west showing Karna
the god of love shooting an arrow at Shiva. The north library pediments
depict Indra creating rain to put out the fire started by Agni to kill
a naga living in the woods, while Krishna and his brother Agni fire

arrows to stop the rain; the other to the west shows Krishna killing his uncle Kamsa. In the opinion of Glaize these pediments are the first Angkorian tympanums decorated with scenes, and in their remarkable use of stylization and realism make them superior to anything that followed.

The sanctuary is entered by the east door, which is only 3½ feet high, and, inside the entrance chamber (or mandapa), a corridor leads to three towers. Six stairways lead up to a platform, each guarded by two kneeling statues of humans with animal heads. The statues are in fact reproductions, as the orginals were either stolen or placed in museums.

Here the lintels of the four cardinal points are also covered in carvings depicting battling monkeys, the abduction of Sita, Vali and Sugriva, and a wild boar.

Banteay Srei is quite simply a beautiful glowing pink masterpiece of architectural religious narrative. As a standalone monument, it would be outstanding, but as part of the wonderful totality of Angkor it holds its own and its own individuality is its gracious contribution.

BANTEAY SAMRE

CITADEL OF THE SAMRE

The Samre were a mountain people who probably acted as mercenaries, but nothing is known of their connection with this temple. Some twenty years ago these buildings were restored using the anastylosis system but since then neglect and the fury of the Khmer Rouge have taken their toll. The image of the lotus bud is repeated again and again inside and outside and the central sanctuary tower has, on its upper level, some interesting Buddhist scenes which come as a surprise in what is primarily a Hindu structure. Roughly square in plan, with four gopuras, the buildings are beautifully proportioned and the unusual interior moat must have had a mirror-like effect in its heyday.

THE KLEANGS

STOREHOUSE

There are two kleangs, a north and a south, positioned behind the twelve towers of Prasat Suor Prat, their jungle backdrop making them appear somewhat too elegant for such a mundane function as storehouse. Indeed, this attribution has frequently been questioned, since the obvious care taken over thier design and layout suggest something far more elaborate, such as reception halls for visiting foreign diplomats. The absence of religious decoration may be further evidence of such a purpose.

PRASAT KRAVAN

THE CARDOMAN SANCTUARY

An inscription over the door frame of the central tower gives a date of AD 921. These early Hindu brick towers contain some fascinating brick bas reliefs of the gods Vishnu and Laksmi. The buildings contain the only examples of brickwork carving to be seen at Angkor and they depict many aspects of Hindu mythology in their own unique Khmer interpretations. It is thought that this complex was constructed not by the king but by local noblemen. Interestingly there is some evidence that the carvings and interiors were once highly coloured, which further confirms an influence by and reference to Hindu temples on the Indian subcontinent.

The buildings have been resotred and all new brickwork is labelled to differentiate it from original work.

KOBAL SPIEN

UNKNOWN ORIGIN, TENTH CENTURY

These strange early carvings give a glimpse of the strength of the religious conviction of the Khmer people. More commonly known to foreigners as the 'River of a Thousand Lingas', this is an area of riverbed carvings similar to Phnom Kulen, but more peaceful. Kobal Spien is about 19 miles north-east of the Bayon and about 6 miles beyond the temple of Banteay Srei along a good dirt road then 45 minutes walk up a jungle path. Do not wander off the well-trodden paths as there is still a serious landmine problem here. The river eventually appears on your left and the first carvings include a large image of Vishnu. As you continue on, you come to an area with several good images of Rama, Laksmi and Hanuman, and further up some lingas. On the way back down there is a path which follows the river and along this stretch are hundreds of lingas. These eventually lead to a waterfall with a pool below.

Ancient carvings by itinerant monks, at Kobal Spien, known as The River of a Thousand Lingas

SCULPTURE

———◆———

THE EXTRAORDINARY RANGE OF CARVING

Details of carvings
throughout Angkor

A NOTE ON RELIGION

In their earliest times the religion of the Khmer people was animism. Certain forms of this, and certainly the worship of all forms of spirits, can still be seen in modern Cambodia. Nature, animals, mountains, fields, river and, above all, ancestors, all exist in the spirit world. It is both a duty and for their own good that the living worship and nurture these spirits. This concept pervaded first Hinduism and then Buddhism.

Hinduism is the world's oldest extant religion, sharing with Buddhism the belief in reincarnation – one absolute being of multiple manifestations. The law of cause and effect, following the path of righteousness and the desire for liberation from the cycle of birth and death. The word 'dharma', 'that which supports the universe', effectively means any path of spiritual discipline which leads to God. Hindu dharma, as one scholar analogizes, can be compared to a fruit tree, with its roots representing the Vedas and Vedantas, the thick trunk symbolizing the spritual experiences of numerous sages, gurus and sains, the branches representing various theological traditions, and the fruit itself, in different shapes and sizes, the various sects and sub-sects. Hindus believe that there is only one supreme Absolute called Brahman. However, they do not advocate the worship of any one particular deity. The gods and goddesses of Hinduism amount to thousands or even millions, all representing the many aspects of Brahman. Therefore, this faith is characterized by the multiplicty of deities. However, the most fundamental of Hindu deities is the Trinity of Brahma, Vishnu and Shiva – creator, preserver and destroyer respectively. Hindus also worship spirits, trees, animals and even planets.

Prince Siddartha (the future Buddha) was born in *c*.563 BC into the royal family of the Shakyas on the India Nepal border. The baby prince's mother died within days of his birth. Since the child had come to the couple late in life his father was determined to give the prince a life of luxury within an enclosed palace community with no knowledge of poverty, suffering or death. Siddhartha grew up and eventually married still living under the illusions of this epicurean atmosphere. Eventually he became a father but at the same time he ventured out into the wider world, where he saw life as it really is. The shocking confrontation of this, in contrast with his own unreal existence led him, at the age of twenty-nine, secretly to leave his family and the palace to pursue the life of a homeless wandering monk. It is said he wandered for seven years encountering various teachers and trying many ascetic paths in his search for enlightenment. One day, while meditating under a bodhi tree, where he was subjected to various temptations, the realization of the Four Noble Truths came to him and he at last obtained enlightenment. From then on he started to travel all over India preaching the nature of the Eightfold Path in which a middle way between self-indulgence and self-mortification will finally lead to the libertation of Nirvana. He was joined by five ascetics who became his disciples, eventually becoming the first Bhiksus (monks) of the Sangha, or Buddhist order, which steadily grew larger and larger. After forty-five years of travelling and preaching, the Buddha returned to the foothills of the Himalayas in his eightieth year. The story is that nearing the end of his homeward journey, he was accidentally fed some poisonous mushrooms and died, thus entering Nirvana and ending his cycle of birth, death and rebirth.

From this came Buddhism. Mahayana Buddhism, meaning 'the greater vehicle', is the major branch of Buddhism, splitting off in the first century AD. It centred on the historical story of Guatama Buddha, and a host of supernatural deities called Bodhisattvas, somewhat reminiscent of Hindu belief. According to Mahayana belief, Buddha had led many lives before reaching

A very active shrine
deep within a temple
ruin at Angkor

enlightenment and thus breaking out of the endless cycle of birth, death and rebirth. A large body of texts called the Jakata stories describe his previous lives and it is these stories that feature in many of the Buddhist carvings of the Khmer.

Theravada (or Hinayana) Buddhism means 'the lesser vehicle'. Mahayanists see Theravada Buddhism as a more agnostic philosophical belief than a religion. The ideals of Therevada remain closer to the original concepts of Buddhism, concentrating on meditation, concentration and the Sangha (monastic orders).

It must be understood that in South-east Asia many beliefs have become interwoven. To a Hindu, Guatama Buddha is an avatar (incarnation of a deity) of Vishnu, but Indra, Vishnu and Shiva also exist with Khmer names and are considered protectors of Buddhism. Theravada Buddhism may now have totally eclipsed Hinduism and Mahayana Buddhism in the region but their underlying spiritual teachings have never totally disappeared from Khmer consciousness.

It is fascinating to note so many very early philosophical principles being absorbed into future religions, e.g. the Hindu concept of the Trinity. The route from animism to Buddhism may be easy to follow, yet the startling similarity between some of the stories, beliefs and rituals of Judaism, Christianity and even the much later Muslim creeds and some of those of the Khmer people cannot be overlooked. So maybe religion can be viewed as an organic process in mankind's struggle to achieve a universal understanding of the cosmos he inhabits. And nowhere can this process can be seen in finer detail than at Angkor.

GLOSSARY

———◦◦◦◦◦———

ASRAMA monastery

AMITABHA Buddha of the higher spirit, represented on the headress of bodhisattvas

AMRITA elixir of life, from the churning of the ocean

ANANTA serpent on which Vishnu reclines on the ocean

ANASTYLOSIS a method of restoring a monument by dismantling it and rebuilding the structure using the original materials and methods

APSARAS celestial dancers

ASURA demon with power equal to that of the gods

AVATAR incarnation or manifestation of Vishnu

AVALOKITESVARA, the compassionate bodhisattva, corresponding to the idea of providence, with four arms and carrying the bantteay citadel

BARAY an area of water enclosed within mounds of earth

BAS RELIEF a sculpture in low relief projecting less than half its depth from the background

BODHISATTVA one in the process of becoming a Buddha

BUDDHA the sage who has achieved ultimate wisdom

BRAHMA one of the gods of the Brahmanic trinity – the creator, generally with four faces, mounted on the hamsa (swan or sacred bird)

CHAM an inhabitant of Champa, kingdom of the Hindu civilization on the coast of what is now Vietnam

DEVA a god

DEVARAJA god-king, the essence of royalty, believed to reside in the royal linga

DEVETA feminine divinity

DHARMASALA house of fire or shleter for pilgrims

DHYANA-MUDRA meditative posture of the Buddha (with hands crossed in the lap)

DURGA one of the wives of Shiva

DVARAPALA a guardian of the temple (deva or asura)

GAJASIMHA lion with a snout

GANESHA son of Shiva, god with the head of an elephant

GANGA one of the wives of Shiva (goddess of the Ganges)

GARUDA divine bird with a human body, enemy of the nagas and the mount of Vishnu

GOPURA entry pavilion to the various temple enclosures

HAYAGRIVA secondary god of the family Shiva, represented with the head of a horse

HINAYANA a Buddhist sect (the 'lesser vehicle')

ISHVARA one of the names of Shiva

INDRA Brahmanic god, master of thunder and lightning; his mount is Airavata the elephant (usually three headed)

KALA the head of a monster, supposed to represet one aspect of Shiva

KALI one of the names of the sakti of Shiva

KAMA the god of love

KRISHNA manifestation of Vishnu

KUBERA the god of wealth, dwarfed and deformed, mounted on a mongoose

LAKSMI the wife or sakti of Vishnu

LANGA phallic idol, one of the forms of Shiva

LOKESVARA alternative name of Avalokitesvara

MAHABHARATA grand Hindu epic

MAHAYANA a Buddhist sect (the 'greater vehicle')

MAITREYA future Buddha

MAKARA sea monster with the head of an elephant, who in ornamentation, often disgorges the naga

MERU mountain, centre of the world and residence of the gods

MUCALINDA naga sheltering Buddha in meditation with his fanned heads

NAGARAJA king of the nagas

NAGI female naga

NANDI sacred bull, the mount of Shiva

NIRVANA the ultimate enlightenment and the supreme Buddhist objective

PARINIRVANA the entry of the Buddha to enlightenment, the pose of the statues of the reclining Buddha

PARVATI wife or sakti of Shiva

PHNOM mountain

PRAH sacred

PRASAT sanctuary, in the form of a tower

PREI forest

PURANA historical Indian legend

PURI town

RAKSHASA inferior demon joining with the asuras against the devas

SARASVATI wife of Brahma, goddess of eloquence

SEMA steles (inscribed stones) placed on the axes and corners of Buddhist terraces to define the sacred platform

SHIVA one of the gods of the Brahamanic trinity – the creator and destroyer, mounted on Nandi (the sacred bull) generally with a third frontal eye and a crescent on the chignon, worshipped in the form of the linga

SITA wife of Rama (Ramayana)

SKANDA god of war, son of Shiva, mounted on a peacock or a rhinoceros

SRAH pool

SREI woman

RAKSHASI feminine form of a rakshasa, a cannibal demon

RAMA a manifestation of Vishnu (Ramayana)

RAMAYANA grand Hindu epic, the history of Rama and Sita

RATI the wife of Kama, god of love

RISHI Brahman ascetic

STUPA or CEDEI a funerary or commemorative monument, usually containing the remains of cremation

SUGRIVA king of the monkeys, dethroned by his brother Valin and ally of Rama (Ramayana)

SURYA god of the sun, haloed with a ring of light and mounted on a horse-drawn chariot

TANDAVA dance of Shiva separating the cosmic periods of the creation and destruction of the worlds

TANTRISM Buddhist sect from the Mahayana

TARA feminine energy of Leksvara, similar to the Prajnaparamita

THERAVADA a Buddhist sect (the 'lesser vehicle')

THOM large

TRIMURTI Brahmanic trinity (shiva between Vishnu and Brahma)

TRIPITAKA sacred Buddhist texts

VASUKI the serpent in the churning of the ocean

VAT pagoda

VEDA Brahman rules

VIHARA monastery

VISHVAKARMAN the divine architect, son of Shiva

VISHNU one of the gods of the Brahmanic trinity - the protector. His mount is Garuda and he generally has four arms that hold a disk, a conch, a ball and a club

YAKSHAS genies of good or evil

YAMA god of death and the supreme judge, mounted on a buffalo

INDEX

Entries in *italics* refer to photographs

Agni 97
Angkor Thom 48–55, 58
    causeways 49, 50, 51, 54, 55
    Gate of the Dead 48
    Gate of Victory 48, 64, 72
Angkor Wat 16–43, 63
    causeways 18, 18, 25, 29, 34
    courtyards 19, 28–9, 29
    Hall of Buddhas 40
    staircases 7, 30
apsaras, 30, 31, 31–2, 38, 42–3, 104–5
Avalokitesvara 58, 60
Ayutthaya 44–7, 94
Bangkok, Thailand 44
Banteau Srei, libraries, 97, 97
Banteay Kdei 56–7
Banteay Samre 100
Banteay Srei 94–9
Baphuon 64
Bayon 48, 58–63, 72, 74
    face towers 58–60, 61, 62–3
Brahmanism 12
brick 12, 46, 47, 101
Buddhism 9, 12, 16, 22–3, 27, 58, 108–9

Mahayana 12
    Theravada 12, 44
de Choisy, Abbé 44
devetas 31–2
Dharmaraja 74
Divarakapandita 94
dvarapalas 20, 22
Garudas 64, 67, 71, 81, 87
Glaize, Maurice 9, 50, 58, 79, 96, 98
gopuras 48–51, 49, 52, 53, 56, 57, 88, 93, 96
Greater Vehicle, see Mahayana
Hanuman 102
Hinduism 12, 22–3, 24, 27, 58, 108
Indra 24
Indravarman VII 72
inscriptions 12, 79, 88
irrigation 12, 16, 25
Isvarapura 94
Jayavarman VII 48, 58, 60, 64, 74, 79, 88
Jayavarman VIII 59
Khmer architecture 18, 22
Khmer civilization 9, 10, 12
Khmer Rouge 100
kleangs 100
Kobal Spien 102–3

Krishna 97–8
Laksmi 101, 102
laterite 12
lingas 94, 102
Lokesvara 58, 93
Mahayana 12, 109
Malraux, André 94
map 14–15
Mekong River 16
Meru, Mount 12, 18, 24, 36
monks 8, 16, 33, 109
Monuments du groupe d'Angkor (Glaize) 9
Mouhot, Henri 10–12, 11
Mucalinda 23, 59
naga balustrades 21, 22, 22–3, 23, 64, 86
Park, Mungo, 10
Phimai, Thailand 56
Phnom Kulen 102
Phnom Penh 44
Prasat Kravan 101
Prasat Suor Prat 72–3, 100
Preah Khan 78–87, 88
    causeways 78–9, 80–1, 83
    Dharmasala 79, 81, 84
    Hall of Dancers 81
    Pavilion 79, 81
Preah Ko 18

Rajendravarman, King 94
Rama 102
Ramathibodi, King 44
Ravana 97
rediscovery 10–13
sandstone 12, 94, 98, 99, 99
Shiva 18, 81, 88, 94, 97
shrines 2, 9, 41
Siddartha 92, 108
Siem Reap 12, 16
Sukhothai 44
Suryavarman II 16–18
Ta Phrom 13, 79, 88–94
    Hall of Dancers 91
Terrace of the Elephants 8, 64–71, 72
Terrace of the Leper King 64, 74–7
Theravada 44, 109
Tonle Sap 16
Travels in Siams, Cambodia and Laos (Mouhot) 10
UNESCO 9
Vaisnavism 18
Vishnu 18, 35, 81, 101, 102
World Monuments Fund 79
Yajnyavahara 94
Yama 74
Zhou Daguan 16, 60–1